Scenarios In Self-Defense

Mary Brandl   Anita Bendickson

Illustrations by Jason Novak

For information or additional copies, contact:

BPS COMMUNICATIONS, LLC
3524 16TH AVE SOUTH
MINNEAPOLIS, MN, 55407-2306

www.bpscom.com

The authors and publishers cannot be held responsible for any loss or damage arising from any information contained in this handbook.

To our mothers,
Margaret Bendickson and Hazel Brandl,
for their love and support, and for giving us
role models of strength, integrity and compassion.
To our Sensei, Robert Fusaro, a master in Karate,
who has given us much more than physical skill.
His teaching embodies a philosophy of
respect for oneself and for others.

ISBN 1-878479-00-8

Library of Congress Catalog Card Number: 89-82386

Revised
Sixth Printing: October, 2009

CONTENTS

1   Introduction

What Is Self-Defense?

Self-Defense: Chances are that just reading the words brings up all sorts of preconceptions...and misconceptions.

For many, even thinking about self-defense activates feelings of fear, vulnerability, even inadequacy. You may feel physically or emotionally incapable of defending yourself. You may think of effective self-defense as something which only highly-trained martial arts experts can master. You may think of self-defense as a set of physical tools – eye-gouging or karate chops – that let you heroically overpower or disable an adversary the way we so often see on television or in the movies.

Unfortunately, these *preconceptions often keep us from thinking constructively about our own safety.*

A Working Definition

Self-Defense, when stripped of its emotional baggage, is quite simply

- *any available means of safely avoiding or escaping a potentially dangerous encounter.*

It needn't involve fighting, or even a direct physical encounter. It needn't involve heroic acts or deeds of daring.

In a self-defense situation, our goal is not to "win", but rather to get away from a potentially dangerous situation safely.

What You'll Learn

This *Scenarios In Self-Defense* program is designed to help you explore and expand your own capabilities and self-defense options.

Scenarios In Self-Defense is probably quite different from any other resource you've encountered. Rather than focusing on a single component of self-defense (like prevention tips or karate-like attacks and releases), the primary emphasis here is on ways to minimize problem encounters *before* things escalate.

While prevention tips certainly can be helpful in avoiding potentially dangerous situations, they are of little value once an encounter is underway.

While physical techniques may be your only hope should an attack turn into a violent physical struggle, reliance on physical moves may mean letting an attacker get close when keeping distance would have been a far safer alternative. *Scenarios In Self-Defense* addresses both prevention and physical resistance, but the most valuable self-defense tools you'll find here will probably involve early intervention and de-escalation; learning to defuse a situation before it reaches the point where physical techniques are your only remaining option.

By understanding the ways in which attacks happen, and that regardless of your physical stature or ability, you *do* have a degree of power in *any* situation, *you can learn to avoid or defuse many of these potentially threatening situations.*

Even more importantly, *you can learn to trust your own feelings and perceptions.* By learning to trust your feelings, you are empowered to act. You stop worrying about hurting the feelings or ego of a potential attacker, and begin to take care of your own feelings.

Rather than waiting for situations to escalate to violence, *you can learn to use your feelings to help you take control of situations early,* at the point where you can still act without great risk of physical injury.

The ideas contained in *Scenarios In Self-Defense* have proven helpful for thousands of men and women who have attended our workshops or seen us on television. They have been put to use by law enforcement officials and security personnel. We hope they'll be helpful for you as well.

Mary Brandl   Anita Bendickson

WARNING

This program is designed to help you <u>maximize</u> your chances of escaping a situation safely. While the authors believe that the material presented in *Scenarios in Self-Defense* may help you to exercise a greater degree of control in a self-defense situation, adherence to the ideas expressed here <u>is not</u> a guarantee of safety. Because the situations and circumstances of assaults are infinitely variable, only YOU can decide when and if these ideas may help you in a unique encounter.

2 The Psychology Of Attacks

Attackers have a natural advantage over victims.

The attacker has taken the initiative, and at least initially, controls the situation. He or she knows just what is going on. He or she is the aggressor.

The victim, on the other hand, may be caught off guard, surprised, even confused. Often, attacks can progress to a critical point before a victim even knows that an attack is under way.

When we, as victims, realize that something is wrong, we must act quickly to take the initiative ourselves. In many cases, acting to take the initiative will disrupt and confuse the attacker enough to allow us time to escape.

In most cases, acting to take the initiative does not mean resisting physically. It means asserting your rights, your power, in an attempt to *avoid* a physical encounter.

Attackers Use Scenarios

Most attackers have thought out their actions to some degree. They have developed a *scenario* – either conscious or unconscious – of how their attack will proceed. This is true whether the attacker is a stranger or someone you *thought* was a close friend.

An attacker's scenario may take many forms. It may involve finding someone who appears to be an easy victim. It may be a means of approach, like asking for a match or the time. It may have to do with isolation, getting a potential victim to a place where help is not available. It may be all of these or any of dozens of other scenario components.

This scenario is every attacker's security blanket, his or her assurance that the attack is going "well".

Disrupting The Attack Scenario

By disrupting an attacker's scenario, you put yourself on more even ground with your attacker. Now the attacker is no longer confident that things are going as planned. You have exploited the *attacker's* weakness – the need to have total control over the situation – and asserted your own strength.

This simple act of disrupting a scenario is enough to defuse many potentially dangerous situations. If you refuse to be an easy victim, your attacker may just back off and wait for someone who will play by his or her rules.

You Need Scenarios, Too

To disrupt an attacker's scenario, you need scenarios of your own. A moment of crisis is not the time to plan a defense. While you will probably need to adjust your scenarios to fit the unique conditions of a particular crisis, having some basic scenarios of your *own* can make you more powerful and more decisive.

By thinking ahead, anticipating what options you may have, you can dramatically increase your chances of effectively disrupting an attacker's scenario.

Thinking ahead and developing your own scenarios is not paranoid or negative thinking. It is a positive step toward feeling less vulnerable, more in control of your own life.

The Components Of Your Personal Self-Defense Scenario

Developing your own scenarios means exploring your options throughout the process of an attack, from prevention to physical resistance. An effective self-defense scenario has three basic components:

- **Prevention/Avoidance** – ways of reducing the likelihood of an attack.

- **Middle Ground Self-Defense** – ways of interrupting attackers' scenarios during the early stages of an attack.

- **Physical Resistance** – absolute last resorts if avoidance and de-escalation fail.

At the back of this book, you'll find a worksheet you can use to explore some self-defense scenarios of your own.

Over the course of this *Scenarios in Self-Defense* program, you'll encounter many options which you might use as building blocks for your own self-defense scenarios. Some will feel better than others to you, so you'll need to incorporate those that work best for *you*.

Remember

You don't need every option to get out of a situation safely.

You do, however, need to be prepared to take the initiative and interrupt your attacker's scenario. Use the material in *Scenarios in Self-Defense* to develop your own scenarios... just in case.

3 Prevention...
And Its Limitations

Historically, "Prevention" has been the quick fix for anyone looking for self-defense information. Most of these rules are probably very familiar to you, but they bear repeating.

On The Street

- After dark, stay in well-lit areas; avoid doorways, shrubbery, shadows and other places where attackers might hide.

- If possible, walk with a friend.

- If you've gotten a ride or taken a cab, ask the driver to wait until you are safely in your car or home.

- Avoid deserted laundromats or apartment house laundry rooms.

- Be cautious about revealing cash or credit cards.

In Your Car

- Keep car doors locked and windows rolled up most of the way.

- Never pick up hitchhikers

- If someone tries to break into your car while you're inside, honk the horn in short, repeated blasts.

- If you are being followed, do not go home. Drive to the nearest police station, fire station, hospital emergency room, gas station or convenience store – anywhere where there are likely to be other people.

- Do not travel at night if you are low on gas or have been experiencing car trouble.
- Park your car in well-lit areas and lock up, even if you'll only be gone for a moment.
- If you must leave car keys with garage or parking lot attendants, leave car keys only, not house keys. Remember: keys can be quickly and easily duplicated.
- Check the back seat and floor of your car before you get in.

At Home

- A woman living alone is safer using only her first initial and last name on mailboxes and in phone directories.
- Be cautious around elevators. If someone on an elevator makes you feel uncomfortable, wait for the next elevator. Get off at the next floor if someone seems odd or threatening.
- Change old locks in a new apartment. Get deadbolts, security chains and peepholes... and *use* them.
- Check ID's when repairmen, salespeople, police or meter-readers come to your home. You are not obligated to let these people into your home, even if their ID seems legitimate. Don't hesitate to phone for confirmation of their identity.
- Instruct children and babysitters not to give out information about who is home or how long someone may be out.
- If you suspect your home may have been burglarized, don't go inside and don't alert any potential intruder to your presence. Call the police from the nearest safe place.
- Don't hide spare keys outdoors. They are too easy to find.
- Lock doors and windows. At night, draw the shades and leave a few lights on.

Some Limitations On The Rules School Of Self-Defense

The rules are all very good advice, of course...but...if you look closely, you'll find that almost all the prevention tips are variations on one of these two important rules:

- Keep out of spaces where attackers are.

or

- Secure your space to keep attackers out.

If we could always do both these things, we would *certainly* be much safer. Unfortunately, we'd also be very lonely and bitter in our sunless, self-imposed prisons of solitary safety.

You see, the rules assume that an attacker will be a stranger. In fact, the vast majority of sexual assaults are by an acquaintance.

The rules assume that we can *stay away* from places where an attacker might be. *We can't.* The reality is that you're more likely to be assaulted in your own home than anywhere else.

The rules don't give you any "what-if" answers. During a real assault, the rules are great for hindsight, but not much good for escaping.

This is not to say that the rules should be ignored. You'll need to choose the rules which you can follow comfortably, and to understand the risks of those rules which you choose not to follow.

Clearly, though, the rules are not enough...

11

4   Middle Ground Self-Defense: Acting Early

Attackers Need To Get Close To Attack

Attackers want to get close. The first part of their scenario depends on it.

Most attackers' scenarios include ploys or approaches which allow them to get within hand-shaking distance, without signaling the potential victim that an attack is starting.

Getting inside this critical distance makes it much easier for the attacker to control the victim both physically and psychologically.

Even an attacker using a weapon almost invariably moves in *before* wielding the knife or gun.

Ploys and approaches which use normal patterns of social behavior help the attacker allay the potential victim's possible suspicions.

These ploys may involve casual verbal approaches. Especially when the potential victim can see the person approaching, these types of ploys can allow the attacker to engage and move in smoothly:

"Do you have change …"

"Don't I know you…"

"Can you give me directions? (the time, etc)"

Many attackers prefer to approach from behind. From a physical point of view, it is less risky. If the potential victim doesn't see the attack coming, it is more difficult to react effectively.

It can also be easier psychologically to approach from behind, because it is then easier for the attacker to see the potential victim as an object rather than as a person.

The attacker can actually get close enough to grab before the victim realizes their intent.

Attackers *want* something from you – your money, your body, your life, your fear – and they can't get it from a distance.

Trust Your Feelings

People communicate in ways we sometimes overlook. When we talk to someone, we share much more than words.

Tone of voice, eye contact, and body language all provide far more information... far more quickly.

Victims often report that something made them feel "uneasy" even before the attack began. This seems to be especially true when the assailant is a stranger.

The most useful thing you can do to upset an attacker's scenario and regain the initiative is to *trust your feelings*.

Feelings come from somewhere. While you may not always understand them, you know when you have them.

Your uneasy feeling about a person does *not* mean that he or she is an attacker. Something, though, is going on that makes you feel uneasy.

You don't need to wait to find out *why* you feel uneasy before acting!

Often, trusting your feelings may mean overcoming some of your social conditioning. You're taught that people are innocent until proven guilty.

Acting on your feelings does not mean passing judgment on the other person. It is taking care of yourself!

Set A Boundary

To interrupt a casual approach, set an unmistakable boundary, using:

- Distance

- Strong Body Language

- Assertive Verbal Responses

By using one or more of these three options, things are no longer ambiguous. You make it impossible for an attacker to continue without tipping you off.

If you say, "Stay over there", and the other person *doesn't*, you know far more about the situation than you did a moment before.

If setting a boundary is ineffective, you should be willing to *get attention*, by whatever means available. Someone who has crossed a clearly-set boundary has *already* proven that your "funny" feelings are right.

Distance

If you don't feel right about a person or situation, get some distance. You don't need anyone's permission to move away when you're feeling uncomfortable.

When you think of keeping distance, don't assume that an attacker will always be a stranger.

In acquaintance situations, the attacker may check out a potential victim over a period of time, gradually invading your space, your personal "comfort zone". Keeping your space for yourself may be enough to discourage a more serious situation later.

Strong Body Language

Attackers often choose victims who appear confused or unaware of what is going on around them. Attackers search for people who appear tense or frightened.

It makes sense – why should an attacker approach someone who looks aware and confident?

Using strong body language when a situation is feeling "wrong" can minimize the possibility of an attack by changing how the attacker perceives you.

Breathe. To use strong body language, put yourself in a position in which you can take a deep breath easily. If you can take a good, deep breath, you are probably in a strong body position. You'll look stronger to others and feel stronger yourself.

Feet Apart. For the strongest position, place your feet apart, a hip's width side to side, and some space between them front to back. This is like having your heels on the diagonal corners of a square.

Relax. Relax your joints, especially knees, elbows and shoulders. This will help you feel more grounded, more stable.

Body Upright. Put your shoulders directly over your hips. For most people, this means bringing your shoulders back. Bring your head back so that your ears are right above your shoulders. Try it. Your body feels centered, balanced, strong.

Figures 1 and 2
Strong Body Position

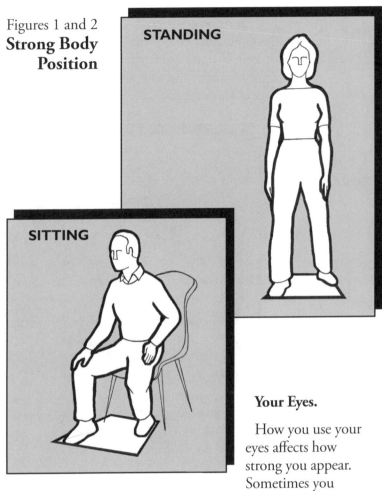

STANDING

SITTING

Your Eyes.

How you use your eyes affects how strong you appear. Sometimes you avoid looking at people who make you feel uncomfortable. You don't want to invite them to start a conversation with you.

As much as you may want to ignore someone who makes you nervous, you need to realize that doing so makes approaching you easier.

You *can* look at someone without making it easy for him or her to talk to you. Center your gaze in the triangle made up of the area between their eyes and shoulders.

Figure 3
Centering Your Gaze

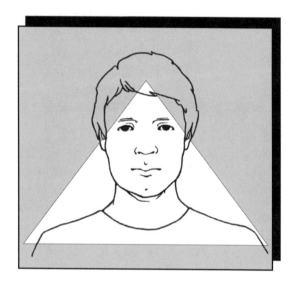

By doing so, you let a potential attacker know you are very aware of him or her, without establishing communication.

Direct eye-to-eye contact may be precisely what the attacker is seeking. Eye-to-eye contact provides a connection, an opportunity to engage you socially.

Less direct contact helps you keep some psychological and emotional distance.

Your Feelings. Strong body language can help you feel stronger emotionally. It makes it more difficult for an attacker to pick up on your fear or anger. Attackers often look for these emotional responses as cues to continue a scenario.

Assertive Verbal Responses

If your goal is to end an encounter which makes you feel uncomfortable, the less emotional and psychological interaction between you and the source of your discomfort, the better.

If a verbal response is called for, using commands and statements in a firm but non-challenging tone is perhaps your most valuable response for ending a situation.

The strong body language described earlier can help you establish that tone physically. When you stand upright, you can speak from the diaphragm (just below your ribs). Using these muscles rather than speaking from the throat can make your voice much stronger and firmer.

Use Commands and Statements. Don't give your attacker easy opportunities to grab onto something you say. Use simple statements and commands which refer only to what "I want" or "I don't want". (Examples: "I want you to take me home." "I don't want to fight with you.")

Try to make your statements as firm as you can, without being insulting. While a person may *deserve* an insult, it probably will do little to improve the situation. Statements which are argumentative or derogatory sometimes work to end an encounter, but they also may escalate things. (Examples: "You are a real jerk." "You can't hurt me.")

You Don't Need To Explain. In acquaintance situations especially, you may be drawn in to giving reasons for your feelings and behavior. By doing so, you prolong the very situation you wish to avoid. You also may feel pressured into prolonging a situation if the "reasons" for your feelings aren't good enough.

You can acknowledge that a person has a different perspective and still stick to what *you* want. (Example: "I realize you feel upset, but I still want to go home.")

You are not obligated to give reasons for your feelings. You don't even need to *have* reasons! Your feelings are real, and they *are* enough.

Get Attention... Make A Scene

When in doubt, publicize your feelings.

If using *strong body language* and *assertive verbal responses* to set a boundary aren't effective, you may want to make a scene in order to get attention.

You can't be sure anyone will come to your aid, but your attacker can't be sure either. Attackers often retreat when things become too public, even if no help has arrived yet.

Yelling. Yelling is an excellent way to publicize your problem. Be sure you yell something which makes it clear that *you want outside help.* Simply yelling "help" may not be your strongest option. Instead, try something like:

"Someone call the police! I need help!"

5   Physical Resistance

While most situations can be averted early, there are times when physical resistance may be the only chance you have to get away safely.

The techniques discussed in this section of *Scenarios In Self-Defense* are very serious and can cause grave injury. These techniques should be used only when you believe there is no other means of escape.

Keep in mind that using physical violence *can put you at greater risk.* Therefore, if you decide to respond physically, it is imperative that you make your strike as effective as possible. Give it everything you've got. The techniques discussed here will show you how.

If you have committed to a physical response, you must be willing to injure your attacker. Never attempt a physical response half-heartedly. You may simply annoy your attacker.

Your goal is to make it physically difficult for your attacker to continue the assault. That means temporarily disabling your attacker, so that you have time to escape.

Release Techniques

Many self-defense training guides concentrate on release techniques, usually adapted from one of the martial arts. While knowing some step-by-step releases may be very helpful, we don't recommend them as your primary means of resisting physically. Here's why.

Understanding and using releases requires training and practice. Even with proper training and execution, a release may not give you time to get away. Your attacker may strike you or grab you again.

Struggling against an attacker's grip is the first thing he or she expects. The grip is your attacker's strong point. It is the focus of the attacker's attention. Getting away may be easier if you concentrate on your attacker's weak areas.

A release does not disable your attacker. To an attacker who is bigger or faster than you, a release may be simply a temporary annoyance. It does not slow an attacker down or prevent pursuit.

Effective physical resistance doesn't mean step-by-step, numbered moves for specific situations. Rather, what you need is an understanding of your strong points and your attacker's weak points.

By understanding your strengths and your attacker's weaknesses, you can react to any situation, even a grip that you've never encountered before.

Your Strengths

Regardless of your size or condition, you have strengths. To get the maximum effectiveness out of your capabilities, the following three concepts are critical:

- **Keep a strong base**
- **Use the stored energy of arms and legs**
- **Use your best weapons**

Let's explore each of these more closely.

Keep A Strong Base

Putting force or energy into a strike is difficult if you need that energy for balance.

To use your body most effectively, you need a strong base, with your weight centered and low. To accomplish this, *get your feet apart and bend your knees slightly.*

By doing so, you can use your weight in a strike without feeling off balance yourself.

Think of using the strong body position discussed in the section on body language (page 16), and examine Figure 4 on the next page. This position *looks* strong because it *is* strong.

You can use this strong body position in one of two ways:

- Step into a strong position *as* you strike.
- Start from this strong position and *rotate your hips and body* into your strike.

Figures 4 and 5
**Strong Base/
Weak Base**

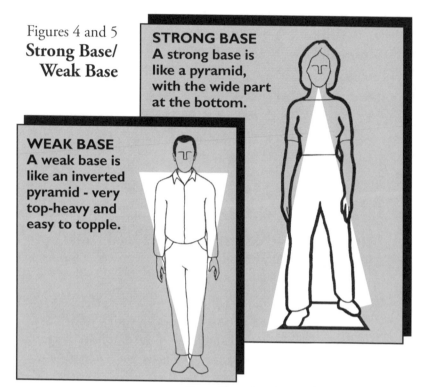

STRONG BASE
A strong base is like a pyramid, with the wide part at the bottom.

WEAK BASE
A weak base is like an inverted pyramid - very top-heavy and easy to topple.

Even if you're sitting down, you can maintain the same strong base. *Spread your feet and sit upright!*

Using Your Feet. If you choose to use one of your feet to kick or stomp, you will obviously be left with only one foot on the ground. Whenever you kick or stomp, *try to keep your balance by:*

- Keeping your body straight. Don't lean toward or away from your attacker.

- Keeping your support leg bent slightly.

- If possible, grabbing your attacker. His or her base can help you keep your balance as you kick (see Figures 7 and 8).

Use The Stored Energy Of Arms And Legs

Swinging an arm or leg is not nearly as rapid or powerful as *uncoiling* it.

When you swing an arm, you strike with the weight of the arm. When you uncoil it from a position close to your body and rotate your hips in the direction of the strike, you add the weight of your entire body to the blow (assuming you're in a strong, well-balanced body position).

Your Arms. To strike with your arms, hand or fist, bend your arm at the elbow and pull your fist back by your side (see Figure 6), or around your head.

An arm coiled in either position has a great deal of stored energy. You can unleash that energy by straightening your arm into a strike.

Pulling back with the other arm as you strike adds to this power, and helps you remember to rotate your body into the blow.

The result is a short, compact, powerful strike which is difficult to avoid.

Figure 6
Striking With Arms, Hands Or Fists

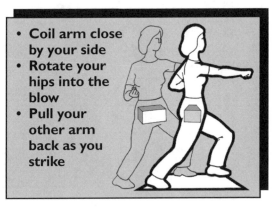

- **Coil arm close by your side**
- **Rotate your hips into the blow**
- **Pull your other arm back as you strike**

Swinging your arm from the shoulder with a straight elbow, on the other hand, is a long, weak blow. Your attacker may have time to react and deflect the blow.

Your Legs. Again, think of coiling for extra power. If you're stomping, coil the leg and drive the foot downward or backward into your target. If you are kicking straight ahead, coil your leg and snap it out and back quickly for extra power. To kick backward, coil and drive the *whole leg* back into the target.

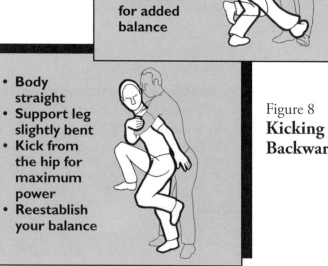

Figure 7
Kicking

- **Body straight**
- **Support leg slightly bent**
- **Snap foot out and back quickly**
- **Grab hold for added balance**

- **Body straight**
- **Support leg slightly bent**
- **Kick from the hip for maximum power**
- **Reestablish your balance**

Figure 8
Kicking Backward

By immediately pulling your leg back, you're prepared to kick again or to reestablish your balance by putting your foot back down.

Use Your Best Weapons

When you choose to respond physically, your goal is to disable, *not* annoy. *Strike only with hard surfaces.*

Think of arms and legs and where they bend. Virtually every joint, when bent or tense, provides a hard striking surface.

Fist – Roll your fingers all the way down, thumb on the outside. You can use the front, back or bottom of the fist to strike. *Never put your thumb inside your fingers!*

Fingers/Nails – Use to *strike* at the eyes. Cup your palm slightly, all five fingers slightly bent and tense. NOTE: Generally, scratching is not disabling, merely annoying.

Heel of Hand – Use to strike *upward*, primarily under the nose or chin. The shorter you are, the more effective this can be!

Outside Edge of the Hand – Use to strike at the neck or backward into the groin, like a "karate chop".

Inside Edge of the Hand – Use the side of the large knuckle on your index finger to strike at the throat. This works best when you have maneuvering room.

Elbows – Use to strike *backward* or to the side, into the ribs or solar plexus.

Knees – Use to strike at the groin. Coil your whole leg back and drive the knee *upward* for maximum effect.

Ball of the Foot – Use to snap out at a knee, shin or ankle. Be sure to bend your toes up out of the way.

Outside Edge of the Foot – Use to stomp down on the instep of an attacker's foot or to scrap down a shin. Make it strong enough to have an effect!

Heel – Use to stomp down onto an instep or to thrust backward into the knee.

Your Attacker's Weaknesses

Regardless of an attacker's size or strength, he or she has weak areas. You have two goals. *Hit 'em where it will count, and hit 'em as hard as you can.*

Once you've committed to a physical response, you *must* follow through by following these two guidelines. If you cannot do so, you are probably better off avoiding physical responses.

Obviously, some of us can strike harder than others. However, if you choose your target carefully, even a fairly weak blow can be very painful and potentially disabling.

For instance, a blow to the throat can make it difficult to breathe, or even rupture the larynx (voice box). A blow to the nose can momentarily blur vision, giving you a chance to escape. A blow up into the groin can make it difficult for your attacker to pursue.

What Targets Are Available?

Basically, your targets can be divided into three main body areas. Generally, the most serious targets are above the shoulders.

The Head

When striking toward the head area, think of the senses first. Next, think of breathing. No attacker can continue for long without a supply of oxygen.

- **Sight** - Into or near the eyes.
- **Hearing** - By clapping *both hands* over the ears you can break an eardrum or even cause a concussion.
- **Smell** - Into or up under the nose.
- **Taste** - Into the mouth or up under the chin.
- **Throat** - Strike either the windpipe, the carotid arteries, or into the hollow of the throat.

The Mid-Body

Mid-body targets are usually less serious. While you may be able to disrupt your attacker's breathing, you are unlikely to cause permanent injury.

- **Solar Plexus** - This soft sensitive nerve area is just below the point where your ribs come together in the center.
- **Stomach**
- **Groin** - Usually kneeing *upward* is more effective than kicking into the groin.

The Lower Body

You can use lower body targets to slow an attacker's pursuit. Of the lower body targets, the knee is the most serious.

- **Knees** - The front, sides and back of the knee can all be effective targets.
- **Shins and Ankles** - Difficult to break bones, but extremely painful.
- **Instep** - The top of the foot is usually more sensitive and less protected than the toes. Bones here are small and breakable.

Figure 9 - **Targets**

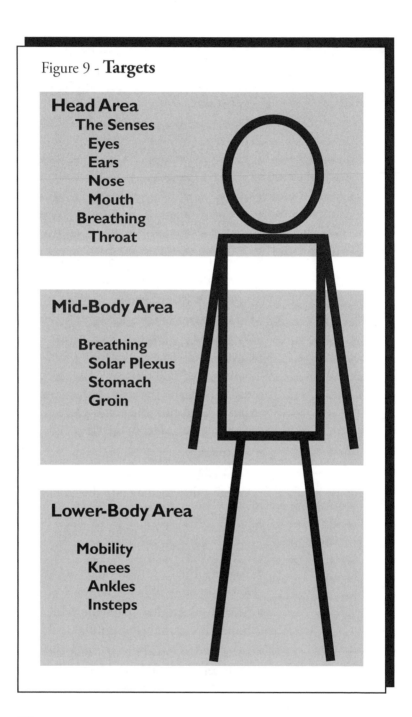

Head Area
    The Senses
        Eyes
        Ears
        Nose
        Mouth
    Breathing
        Throat

Mid-Body Area

    Breathing
        Solar Plexus
        Stomach
        Groin

Lower-Body Area

    Mobility
        Knees
        Ankles
        Insteps

Choosing Weapons And Targets

Of course, you should only choose physical resistance if you feel you have no other options for escaping safely. Considering just how threatened you feel can help you decide what to do.

A very serious and immediate threat - for instance, being choked - calls for the most immediate and drastic physical resistance. Go for the most vulnerable targets you can reach: eyes, throat, or ears, for example.

If the threat is less serious or if help is nearby - for instance, if you've been grabbed by the arm on a city street - you may want to consider something less drastic: an elbow in the ribs or a sharp kick in the shin.

Distance may also play a factor. You can be too close to kick effectively or too far away to stomp and still keep a strong body position.

To identify available targets and weapons, you need to answer two questions.

1. **What do you have free?** Two arms. Two legs. These are your weapons. Which are available?

2. **What targets are available?** What head targets are accessible? What midbody targets? What lower body targets?

If you don't feel the situation warrants delivering a blow *as hard as you can,* choose another less serious target, or forget physical resistance altogether.

Irritating or annoying an attacker is more

31

dangerous than doing nothing. You must be ready to hurt your attacker. After all, he or she appears willing to hurt you!

Keep in mind that you *do* have the legal right to defend yourself from attack in order to get away safely. You *do not*, however, have the right to use excessive force. Use your feelings to judge what responses are appropriate.

About Fear And Panic

The human "fight or flight" response is instinctive. It can help you if you use it constructively.

Fear can actually be helpful. It gives you a burst of adrenaline, a hormone which can help you run faster or hit harder.

Panic, on the other hand, is anything but helpful. It can keep you from thinking straight, considering your options, and acting decisively.

You can avoid being immobilized by panic by using these two techniques:

1. Breathe Deeply - If you start to feel afraid, take a couple of deep breathes. This will help you relax enough so that you can think and move. Holding your breath only deprives you of oxygen and intensifies fear and panic. Yelling can also help you keep oxygen coming.

2. Visualize - As much as possible, try to decide on a few preferred options *in advance.* Visualize how you might escape from different types of situations. The more positive options you have considered, the more resources you'll have at your immediate disposal in a crisis.

6 Weapons: Yours And Theirs

Should You Carry A Weapon?

Only you can decide whether carrying a weapon can make you feel safer.

You should, however, understand the risks and advantages of each type of weapon. For instance, during an assault, the victim is often injured by his or her own weapon.

Never substitute weaponry for common sense. Even if you're carrying mace, a dark alley is not the place to be!

Guns and Knives. In most states, it is illegal to carry a gun or a large knife in your hand or on your person. It is also extremely dangerous. Don't do it!

Stun Guns. A stun gun is a device capable of delivering a momentarily disabling electric shock. Stun guns are unwieldy and hard to use. You must actually hold the stun gun against the skin - in some cases *bare* skin - for several seconds. Stun guns require cooperative assailants.

Mace.* Mace and other brands of eye/ nose irritant spray are somewhat more practical for the average person, but still

---

* *Mace is a tradement of Smith & Wesson Chemical Company.*

might be used against you during an assault. Mace can be effective from "point blank" up to a range of ten or fifteen feet, but it won't always stop assailants who are high, psychotic or enraged. Mace comes in a powerful, pocket-size spray can. Like any spray can, a propellant may leak or the nozzle may become clogged. Mace may also freeze at low temperatures.

Noise Makers. Noise makers are the only weapons which *can't be used against you.* They can be used early in an encounter to attract attention, or later, startling an attacker to provide a chance to strike or escape. The most common are whistles and "shriek alarms". Like mace, many shriek alarms are essentially "spray cans". The same cautions apply. Other alarms use batteries, which should be checked occasionally. If it is possible to also yell when setting off an alarm, do it! Like mace, *a noise maker must be in your hand to be effective!*

Weapons You Already Have. A key can be a very effective weapon. Having keys in your hand is an easy, practical safety measure. Hold one key between your thumb and forefinger, just as if you were opening a door. Choose a key ring that fits comfortably in your hand when you tighten your fist. Pens, pencils, or nail files can also be effective. Aim for a soft part of the body: the groin, throat or eyes. These simple devices can be especially comforting if you aren't confident of your physical abilities. They can make an otherwise weak blow devastating!

Assailants With Weapons

The majority of attackers are unarmed, but as society grows more violent, the possibility of an armed attack has grown as well.

You've probably been advised that when faced with an armed attacker, the best course of action is to simply do what the attackers says.

If the attacker is after your wallet, purse, or car – if the attacker's goal is *material* – this is excellent advice! Don't risk your life for money or credit cards! *They* can be replaced. *You* can't be.

However, if the attacker's intent is to maim or kill you, the situation changes. You are at immediate risk, a strong physical response may actually be *safer* than doing nothing at all.

Consider the following scenarios.

If You Are *Not* Isolated

If you are approached in a shopping mall, on a busy downtown street, or in a parking lot with other people around, you may want to consider acting.

Often, an armed attacker will use a weapon as a means to force you to go somewhere more isolated.

The likelihood that an attacker will actually *use* a weapon *goes up* if he or she can isolate you, and your chances of getting help *go down*.

You probably will have a choice between running and fighting. *Neither* option is risk-free.

If you must strike to break free and escape, choose the most vulnerable target available... and don't wait around to strike again.

Attract as much attention as you possibly can as you strike or retreat. The likelihood that an attacker will use a weapon drops dramatically if he or she is seen by a number of people.

If You
Are
Isolated

If you are alone, an attacker is far more likely to actually use a weapon. Cooperating with the attacker may be the only way to lower the risk of injury.

If the attacker seems agitated, **move slowly** and deliberately, keeping your hands in view. Do not make loud noises or sudden movements. **Reassure the attacker,** in as calm a voice as you can muster, "I'll do what you say, you don't need to use the (weapon/knife/gun)."

Remember to **breathe slowly** to help yourself remain calm, and **wait for an opportunity to escape.**

Make the attacker feel he or she can get exactly what they want... without the weapon. In some cases, the attacker may put a weapon down if a victim seems compliant.

If The
Weapon Is
Used

Guns. If an attacker is armed with a gun, and is *definitely* planning to use it, the only thing you *can* do is create a distraction, either real or imaginary.

The only realistic time to attempt escape or resistance is when the attacker's attention is elsewhere.

If you are close, concentrate on the weapon arm. Keep it pushed away from you. If you have some distance, run for cover, even if it's not the most direct escape route.

Understand, though, that in such a drastic situation, there are *no safe responses*...unless you're playing the title role in a movie.

Knives. If your attacker is stabbing or slashing, get something - anything! - between you and the attacker. If you're inside, a light chair, a lamp, or pillows and cushions can work well. Outside, use anything you're holding: a briefcase, book bag, purse, even a light jacket if it's all you have. A cut on the hand or arm is far less serious than a laceration to the body. Run at the first opportunity, and get attention!

WARNING

Martial arts or self-defense training from a qualified instructor can give you more options when confronted with an armed attacker; however, even the best training cannot eliminate the risk in an encounter. The situations described here are the most drastic imaginable. Nothing an fully prepare you to deal with them. The strategies offered here are absolute final options, and should be attempted only in truly desperate situations. Understand that the risk of injury is extremely high.

7   **Summing Up**

**Early
Intervention
And
De-escalation
Are Your
Best
Defenses**

- **Develop Your Own Self-Defense Scenarios To Help You React Quickly And Effectively**

- **Trust Your Feelings**

- **Set A Boundary Early, Using:**

    1. Distance

    2. Strong Body Language

    3. Assertive Verbal Responses

- **Make A Scene If Necessary**

If You Must Resist Physically, Make It Count

- Use Your Strengths Against Your Attacker's Weaknesses

- Consider What You Have Available: Two Arms, Two Legs

- Consider What Targets Are Available:

  1. *Head Area*

  2. *Mid-Body Area*

  3. *Lower Body Area*

- Choose Targets Based On How Threatened You Feel

Appendix A: Some Sample Scenarios

About These Sample Scenarios

This appendix is designed to show you how others have effectively dealt with potential or very real attacks.

Please take the time to read through these stories and use them as a first step in developing your own self-defense scenarios.

Chances are, some of these stories will bring up memories of your own. They'll ring some subconscious bells. Pay attention to those bells. Your own experiences...both positive *and* negative...can help you build effective scenarios.

Scenario 1: Bernice

Thinking Ahead Gives You Options When You Need Them Most

Bernice was an older woman who lived near the karate studio where the authors teach. She came into the school one afternoon just to look around.

She commented that when she was young, "ladies" didn't do this sort of thing, though now she thought it was a great idea.

She had, in fact, been called upon to make a strong response of her own.

Bernice worked in a nursing home kitchen, and usually walked to work about 6 a.m.

Bernice was not confident in her physical abilities. Arthritis in her knees made it difficult to run. She didn't think she could yell loud enough to wake anyone.

Usually it was dark and the streets were nearly deserted, so she made a habit of carrying one of her hat pins in her hand.

One day as she was walking, a man grabbed her from behind. Since the hatpin (all six inches of it!) was in her hand, she swung it back into the attacker's groin. He let go and didn't follow as she hurried away.

Bernice had only considered one self-defense option… but because she was prepared, she was able to defend herself against a very real assault.

Remember: You don't need every option to get away!

41

Scenario 2: Angela

Trust Your Feelings And Take Care Of Yourself First

Angela was leaving work late one night. Her building was virtually deserted.

As she approached the elevator she saw someone inside. She called, "hold the door" and hurried down the hall.

The man in the elevator stopped the door and waited.

As Angela got closer, she began to feel "funny" about the man in the elevator. She stopped and said "never mind" and turned back toward her office.

The concepts she learned through our workshop helped Angela feel good about acting on her feelings.

Angela described it this way:

"I felt I could make my own choices. I actually felt very, very strong making the choice that, since I felt uneasy, I was perfectly capable of walking away and waiting for another elevator. I didn't feel like I had to get on that elevator with him... and it didn't even bother me. I felt empowered rather than embarrassed."

Remember: You don't need to feel embarrassed about taking care of yourself!

Scenario 3: Kate

Trust Your Feelings And Save The Analysis For Later

Kate is a single parent who lives with her two children in a home on a dead end cul-de-sac. One morning, she was awakened at about 3:00 a.m. by the door bell. When she went to the door, she encountered a young woman.

Keeping her screen door latched, Kate asked the woman what she wanted. The woman explained that she had been visiting friends and that she needed to use the phone because her car had broken down.

Kate hesitated, feeling half-asleep and not at all comfortable about the situation. Finally, she said, "OK, you wait here and I'll call a tow for you."

When Kate returned, the woman was gone! Kate called the police, who found no trace of the woman or the broken down car. They told Kate that her story fit a number of recent robbery scenarios. Had Kate opened the door, a couple of male cohorts would likely have burst in, assaulted Kate and robbed her home.

It wasn't until later that Kate was able to see the *logical* reasons for her discomfort. If the woman was visiting friends nearby, why didn't she go back to *their* house? If the friends were *not* nearby, how did the woman end up on Kate's dead-end street? Kate's social conditioning told her to let the woman come inside. By trusting her feelings instead, Kate probably avoided serious injury.

Remember: Usually feelings have some basis, even if it's not instantly obvious.

43

Scenario 4: Sam

Strong Body Language Can Help You Look Aware And Confident

Sam was taking the freeway home from work one unusually congested rush hour. Everyone seemed irritated and impatient.

When a truck tried to cut in on Sam, he sped up and the truck was forced to move in behind. Sam thought nothing of it…

…until he exited the freeway, and the truck zipped past Sam and forced him off onto the shoulder. As Sam stopped his car, the driver of the truck came charging back toward Sam's car, yelling obscenities as he approached.

Sam, who has had several years of karate training, got out of his car, sensing that this was a situation he might handle better on his feet.

Realizing that nothing he could say would help the situation, Sam didn't respond verbally. Instead, he stepped back into a strong stance: feet apart, knees flexed, head up and body straight.

The trucker immediately stopped moving in, but continued his string of profanities as he headed back to his truck. A moment later he returned, this time carrying a tire iron.

Sam maintained his silent stance, angry himself, but determined not to give the truck driver anything to feed his anger.

The truck driver punctuated his curses with menacing swings of the tire iron, but continued to stay well back.

Finally, unable to get Sam to react, the trucker stopped, stormed back to his car and drove off.

Remember: Looking strong can help you feel stronger.

Scenario 5: Clara And Angie

Assertive Verbal Language Is A Middle Choice Between Passive And Aggressive Responses

Clara and Angie were college roommates living off-campus together. Their apartment was nice, but to get rent they could afford, they had to live in an area known for prostitution and other problems.

Because they both had evening jobs, they tried to take the bus home together whenever possible.

One evening, as they were walking the two blocks from the bus stop to their building, a very fancy car began following them slowly down the street.

At first, Clara and Angie tried to ignore the car and walk faster. The car pulled up alongside the two young women, and a man sitting on the passenger side rolled down his window and said, very suggestively, "Hey ladies, we sure wouldn't mind giving you a lift. Come on in."

Angie reacted aggressively, swearing at the man and yelling "NO WAY."

The man got out of the car, saying he would "teach them a lesson."

Ignoring the car hadn't worked, and Angie's aggressiveness had actually worsened the situation.

Clara put up her hands, palms out, and addressed the guy getting out of the car. "Look," she said, shaking her head, "we really don't need a ride. We're just walking home." She kept her voice quiet and calm.

To their surprise, he grumbled, "All right, then," and got back into the car, which took off with a squeal.

Remember: When using assertive verbal responses, concentrate on what YOU want or need.

45

Appendix B: Your Own Self-Defense Scenarios

How To Use The Personal Self-Defense Scenario Worksheet

The worksheet on the following pages can help you think constructively about your own self-defense scenarios, but it is only a starting point.

Completing the worksheet (and developing other scenarios) is a four-step process.

1. **Identify a situation.** We've included several hypothetical situations. Incidentally, each of the situations listed *has* led to a real attack.

2. **Prevention.** Try to come up with ways by which the situation might have been avoided entirely...*before* an attacker was even in sight. Use common sense and be practical. You may want to refer to some of the tips listed on pages 9 and 10.

3. **Avoidance and De-escalation.** It is not always possible to avoid situations entirely. Try to think of ways in which you might have acted early in the situation to stop the attacker from getting close, or to keep the attacker from viewing you as a potential victim. Consider strong body language, verbal commands, distance, etc. You may want to review pages 12-20.

4. Physical Resistance. It is not always possible to defuse a situation early. Now consider the situation as *very* serious. You must use physical resistance to avoid being injured. It may help you to visualize the situation further: how are you being held, what do you have free to defend yourself? Consider what techniques you could use, what target areas you would use, and how you could maximize the effectiveness of your strike. You may want to refer to pages 21-32. (Physical resistance may not be appropriate in every situation).

As you complete the worksheet, *be as specific as you possibly can!*

You have just left a bar where you were socializing with friends. As you walk through the parking lot to your car, you hear someone walking behind you. As you get close to your car, he calls out: "Hey, you. Got a match?" As you fumble in your pocket, he pushes you down and grabs your wallet.

PREVENTION _____

_____

_____

_____

_____

_____

_____

_____

_____

_____

_____

AVOIDANCE & DE-ESCALATION _____

_____

_____

_____

_____

_____

_____

_____

PHYSICAL RESISTANCE

You are riding your bike down a pleasant parkway on your way home. A van approaches from behind, coming very fast and swerving in close to you, almost forcing you off the road. The people in the van shout at you as they go by. About a half a block ahead of you, the van pulls over and stops.

PREVENTION _____

_____
_____
_____
_____
_____
_____
_____
_____
_____

AVOIDANCE & DE-ESCALATION _____

_____
_____
_____
_____
_____
_____
_____

PHYSICAL RESISTANCE

You are at home in bed. It is 3:30 in the morning. You are awakened by the sound of glass breaking. You are pretty sure someone has broken into the house... but everything seems quiet.

PREVENTION —————————————————————

———————————————————————————

———————————————————————————

———————————————————————————

———————————————————————————

———————————————————————————

———————————————————————————

———————————————————————————

———————————————————————————

———————————————————————————

AVOIDANCE & DE-ESCALATION ————————

———————————————————————————

———————————————————————————

———————————————————————————

———————————————————————————

———————————————————————————

———————————————————————————

———————————————————————————

———————————————————————————

PHYSICAL RESISTANCE ———————————

You meet an interesting man from another department at work. After talking casually for several weeks, he invites you to lunch. It was very pleasant, so you agree to join him for a movie the next night. On the way to the movie, he stops the car at an isolated park and tries to get intimate with you.

PREVENTION _____

_____

_____

_____

_____

_____

_____

_____

_____

AVOIDANCE & DE-ESCALATION _____

_____

_____

_____

_____

_____

_____

PHYSICAL RESISTANCE

You are in the laundry room of your dorm. It is late Saturday afternoon and the dorm is mostly deserted. You are reading a magazine while you wait for the dryer to finish. A man comes in. He looks a little old to be a student living in the dorm, and he has no laundry with him. He tries to start a conversation with you.

PREVENTION _____

_____

_____

_____

_____

_____

_____

_____

_____

_____

AVOIDANCE & DE-ESCALATION _____

_____

_____

_____

_____

_____

_____

_____

_____

_____

_____

_____

_____

_____

_____

_____

_____

PHYSICAL RESISTANCE ————————

_____

_____

_____

_____

_____

_____

_____

_____

_____

_____

_____

_____

_____

ABOUT THE AUTHORS

Mary Brandl and **Anita Bendickson** are speakers, instructors and consultants in self-defense and strategies for managing confrontation.

They have instructed hundreds of groups and organizations. These have included individuals and groups with specialized situations, such as seniors, people with physical or mental disabilities, and those whose jobs involve confrontation.

Mary and Anita hold 4th and 5th degree black belts respectively, and are registered with the American Amateur Karate Federation and the Japan Karate Association, U.S. They teach traditional Japanese Shotokan Karate through the Midwest Karate Association, Minneapolis/St. Paul.

SCENARIOS IN SELF-DEFENSE DVD

A comprehensive and practical self-defense program offered on DVD, *Scenarios In Self-Defense* consists of:

I. Your Early Options: A demonstration of the use of distance, strong body language, assertive verbal responses and much more as Mary and Anita give you the tools you need to handle stranger situations more effectively. Running time 34:15

II. When An Acquaintance Becomes An Assailant: Mary and Anita explore options for dealing effectively with acquaintances who overstep the bounds. Running time 34:45

III. Practical Physical Resistance: Mary and Anita present a practical approach designed to help you use your strengths against an attacker's weaknesses. It is useful even for individuals with limited physical skills or abilities. Running time 34:30

For information about the DVD, additional copies of this book, or to inquire about workshops/consultations, visit our website at:

www.bpscom.com
or write to:
BPS Communications, LLC
3524 16th Ave South
Minneapolis, MN, 55407-2306

1-800-365-4BPS